BeaN The Coffee Fairy

written by:

Alex H. Singh

USA Today Bestselling Author

illustrations and coffee stains by:

Fabio Oliveria

To all the under-caffeinated adults in need of a smile, a laugh, and a warm cup of coffee to brighten their day.

"Friendship brews in the heart, like coffee in a pot."

In a land not far away, where the sun kisses the morning dew, lived a fairy named, Bean with a mission pure and true. While fairies often frolicked with children, giggling and playing, Bean the Coffee Fairy had different thoughts in his mind, he was swaying.

Bean despised the laughter of children, their playful little games. He thought adults needed him more, to call out their names. With a wand in hand and determination in his eyes so bright, Bean set out on his journey, to make adults' mornings just right.

For in the bustling cities and sleepy countryside, adults stumbled through their mornings, their spirits defied. They yearned for a pick-me-up, to chase away the haze, and Bean knew he was the one to bring the sun's golden rays.

With each flutter of his wings, and each sprinkle of his brew, Bean brought joy to tired souls, his magic shining through. For in every cup of coffee, brewed with love and care, lay the promise of a new day, with endless possibilities to share.

So as Bean soared through the skies, with a smile upon his face, he knew he had found his purpose, in this wondrous place. For though he may be small, his heart was mighty and true, and he would spread his coffee magic, to all who needed a brew.

And thus begins the tale of Bean, the Coffee Fairy bold, whose adventures would warm hearts, as timeless tales unfold. So grab your favorite mug, and settle in for a ride, as Bean's story begins, with joy and laughter by your side.

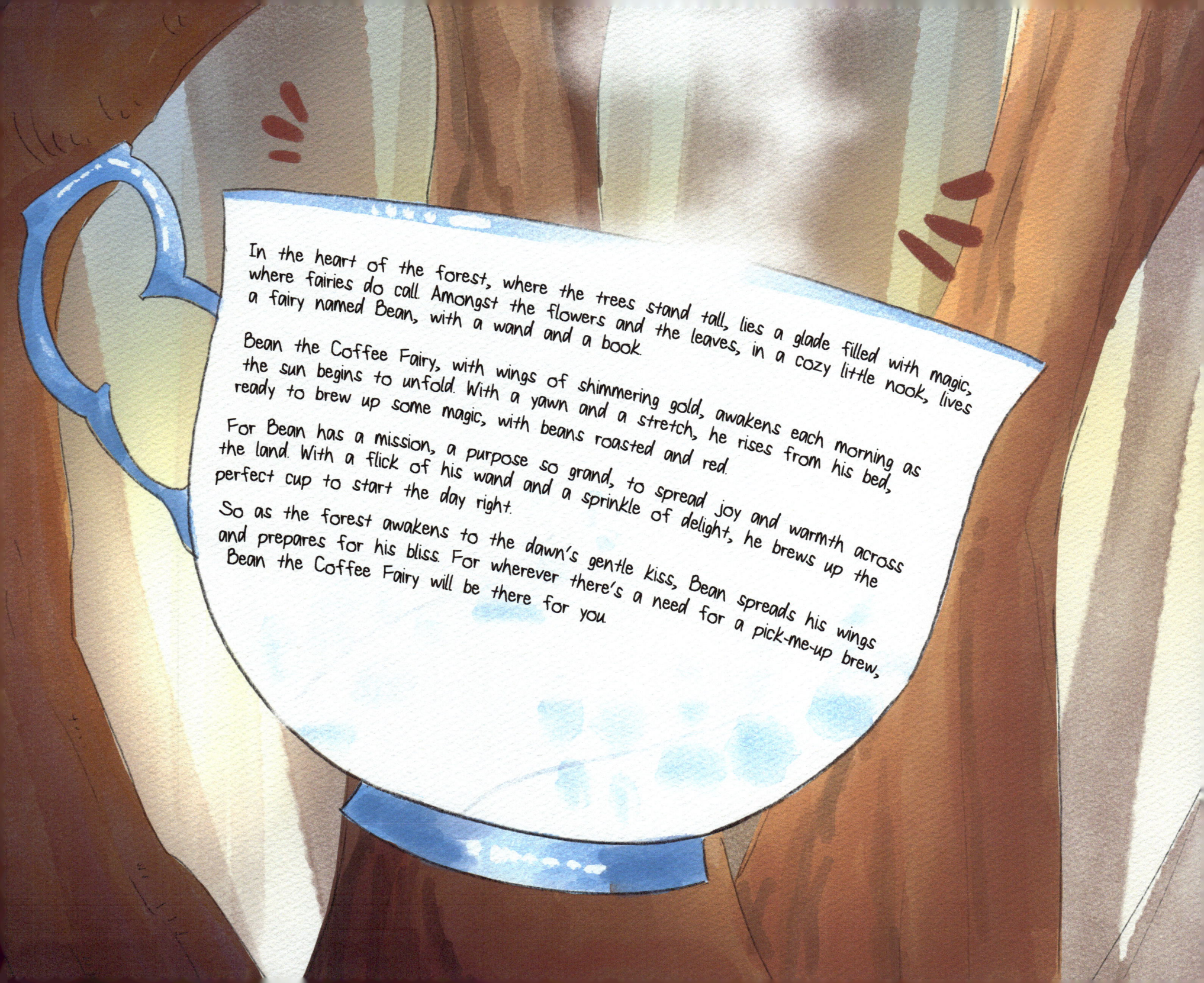

In the heart of the forest, where the trees stand tall, lies a glade filled with magic, where fairies do call. Amongst the flowers and the leaves, in a cozy little nook, lives a fairy named Bean, with a wand and a book.

Bean the Coffee Fairy, with wings of shimmering gold, awakens each morning as the sun begins to unfold. With a yawn and a stretch, he rises from his bed, ready to brew up some magic, with beans roasted and red.

For Bean has a mission, a purpose so grand, to spread joy and warmth across the land. With a flick of his wand and a sprinkle of delight, he brews up the perfect cup to start the day right.

So as the forest awakens to the dawn's gentle kiss, Bean spreads his wings and prepares for his bliss. For wherever there's a need for a pick-me-up brew, Bean the Coffee Fairy will be there for you.

With his apron tied tight and his wand held high, Bean sets off on his quest, reaching for the sky. Through the whispering woods and the babbling brooks, he searches for the perfect beans with curious looks.

In the shade of the trees and the warmth of the sun, Bean roams far and wide, his journey just begun. He meets creatures of all shapes and sizes, each with a tale, and with every step he takes, his determination does not fail.

For Bean knows that with each bean he finds, he brings joy and comfort to all kinds. So, he presses on, through thickets and thorns, his spirit unbroken, his resolve reborn.

In a clearing bathed in sunlight, Bean sets up his brew, with cauldron and wand, he knows just what to do. He gathers the finest beans, roasted to perfection, and with a twinkle in his eye, he begins his caffeinated confection.

With a flick of his wand and a sprinkle of his charm, Bean brews up a potion that could calm any alarm. The aroma fills the air, rich and inviting, and soon, creatures from far and wide come alighting.

They gather around Bean, their cups held high, eager to taste his brew and give a joyful cry. With laughter and chatter, they drink deep and long, and in Bean's magical brew, they find where they belong.

For Bean's brew is more than just coffee in a cup, It's a potion of joy, of friendship, and love's true sup. So, raise your mugs high and let your spirits soar, for with Bean the Coffee Fairy, there's always more in store.

In the heart of the forest, where the trees stand tall, Bean stumbled upon a village, tiny and small. There, in a glen filled with shimmering light, live the Espresso Elves, skilled in coffee's delight.

With their pointed hats and twinkling eyes so bright, they brewed up potions to bring joy and light. Bean watched in wonder as they worked their magic, turning beans into elixirs, so strong and so tragic.

With a smile and a wave, Bean approached the elves, his heart filled with wonder, his spirit swells. They welcomed him warmly, with laughter and song, and together they brewed, all the night long.

With each cup they poured and each story they shared, Bean felt a connection, a bond that flared. For in the company of the Espresso Elves so merry. He found friendship and joy, oh so very.

As the stars danced above and the fire burned bright, Bean knew he had found his place in the night. With the Espresso Elves by his side, he felt free, to spread his magic and brew with glee.

As Bean ventured deeper into the forest so green, he stumbled upon a sight like he'd never seen. A mischievous sprite with a twinkle in his eye, danced among the flowers, under the sky so high.

With a grin on his face and mischief in his heart, the sprite beckoned Bean to play a part. Together they frolicked, through meadows and glades, laughing and dancing beneath the forest's shades.

But as they day turned to dusk and the shadows grew long, the sprite revealed a secret, like the end of a song. For he was no ordinary fairy of the wood, but a trickster who danced where no fairy should.

With a wink and a giggle, he vanished from sight, leaving Bean along in the fading light. But though the sprite may be gone, his laughter still rings, in the heart of Bean, where mischievous joy springs.

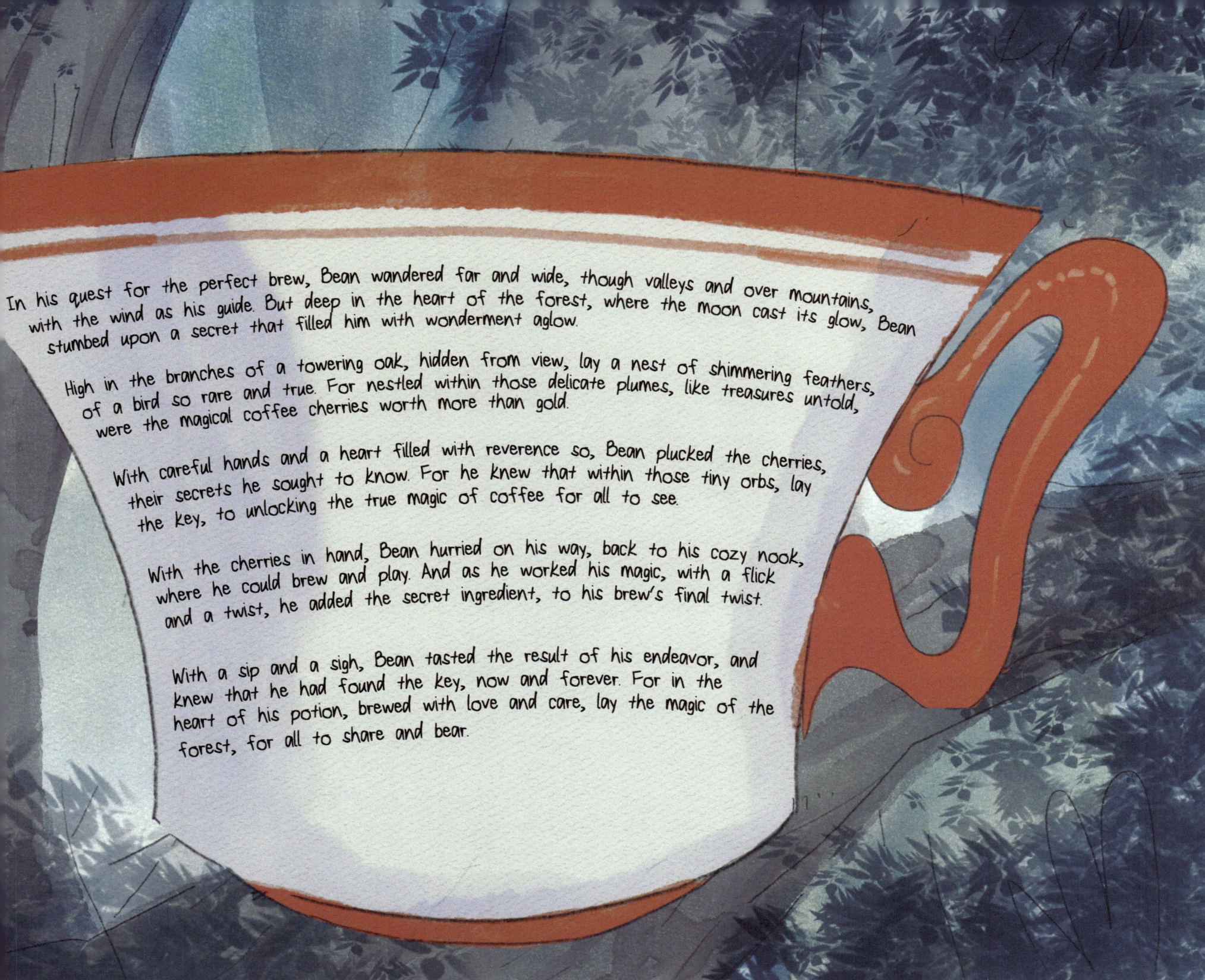

In his quest for the perfect brew, Bean wandered far and wide, though valleys and over mountains, with the wind as his guide. But deep in the heart of the forest, where the moon cast its glow, Bean stumbed upon a secret that filled him with wonderment aglow.

High in the branches of a towering oak, hidden from view, lay a nest of shimmering feathers, of a bird so rare and true. For nestled within those delicate plumes, like treasures untold, were the magical coffee cherries worth more than gold.

With careful hands and a heart filled with reverence so, Bean plucked the cherries, their secrets he sought to know. For he knew that within those tiny orbs, lay the key, to unlocking the true magic of coffee for all to see.

With the cherries in hand, Bean hurried on his way, back to his cozy nook, where he could brew and play. And as he worked his magic, with a flick and a twist, he added the secret ingredient, to his brew's final twist.

With a sip and a sigh, Bean tasted the result of his endeavor, and knew that he had found the key, now and forever. For in the heart of his potion, brewed with love and care, lay the magic of the forest, for all to share and bear.

High above the forest, where the clouds drift by, Bean encountered a spectacle that caught his eye. A band of baristas, with aprons of white, brewing coffee in the sky, with all of their might.

Their espresso machines hummed with celestial song, as they brewed up clouds of coffee, oh so strong. Bean watched in amazement, as they worked with such a grace, turning clouds into cappuccinos, in their heavenly space.

With a smile and a wave, Bean joined in their brew, his wand adding magic to the heavenly view. Together they brewed, with laughter and cheer, bringing joy to the heavens, for all to hear.

As the sun dipped below the horizon, painting the sky with gold, Bean bid farewell to the cloud baristas, his heart bold. For in their company, he found inspiration anew, to spread his magic far and wide, with coffee so true.

In his quest for new flavors, Bean ventured afar, to the Land of Spice, where the skies shimmered like a star. Through valleys of cinnamon and mountains of clove, he journeyed with a purpose and courage, guided by love.

In the bustling markets, where spices filled the air, Bean sought out the rarest treasures, with a determined flair. With each step he took, he felt the magic grow, for in the Land of Spice, there were wonders to show.

He sampled exotic blends, infused with cardamom's delight, and danced with joy in fields of saffron, so bright. But amidst the hustle and bustle, he found a hidden gem, a spice so rare and precious, it made him feel like a gem.

With a twinkle in his eye and a skip in his stride, Bean gathered the spice, his heart filled with pride. For he knew that with this treasure, he could brew, a potion of magic, with flavors both old and new.

As he journeyed back home, through valleys and glades, Bean carried with him the spice, like a gift from the fates. And with each step he took, his heart filled with glee, for he knew that his brew would be a delight for all to see.

ARKET

Deep within the enchanted forest, where the trees whispered secrets old, Bean stumbled upon a hidden grove, were mysteries untold. With moss-covered paths and ivy-clad walls, the grove beckoned Bean with its ancient calls.

As he wandered through the shadows, his heart filled with wonder, Bean discovered a sight that made his heart thunder. For nestled within the grove, bathed in shimmering light, stood a majestic coffee tree, a wondrous sight.

Its branches stretched high, reaching for the sky, bearing cherries of crimson, like jewels so high. With hands trembling with reverence, Bean plucked a cherry so rare, knowing that within its depths lay magic beyond compare.

With careful hands and a heart full of awe, Bean brewed the cherries, with a touch so raw. The potion that emerged was unlike any before, filled with the escence of the forest, pure to the core.

As he sipped the brew, his senses awoke, filled with the magic of the grove, no words to invoke. For in that hidden place, Bean found his truest brew, a potion of wonder, made for me and you.

As Bean delved deeper into the forest's heart, he encountered a darkness, tearing it apart. A shadowy figure, lurking in the night, threatened the peace with its sinister might.

With courage in his heart and magic in his hand, Bean confronted the shadow, taking a stand. With each flicker of his wand, he banished the gloom, bringing light and hope to dispel the doom.

The shadow recoiled, its power waning fast as Bean's light overcame it, lasting and steadfast. With a final burst of magic, the shadow was no more, and peace returned to the forest, as it was before.

With a sigh of relief and a smile on his face, Bean continued with his journey, at a leisurely pace. For though darkness may threaten, he knew he was strong, with the power of friendship and courage lifelong.

In the heart of the enchanted forest, where the fireflies dance, Bean gathered his friends for a magical chance. With a cauldron of dreams and a sprinkle of starlight, he brewed up a potion, shimmering and bright.

With laughter and joy, they gathered around, as Bean poured the brew, with a magical sound. The aroma filled the air, like a sweet melody, as they savored each sip, with hearts full of glee.

For in Bean's brew, they found more than just taste, they found love and friendship, not a moment to waste. With each cup they shared, their bond grew strong, as they danced in the moonlight, all night long.

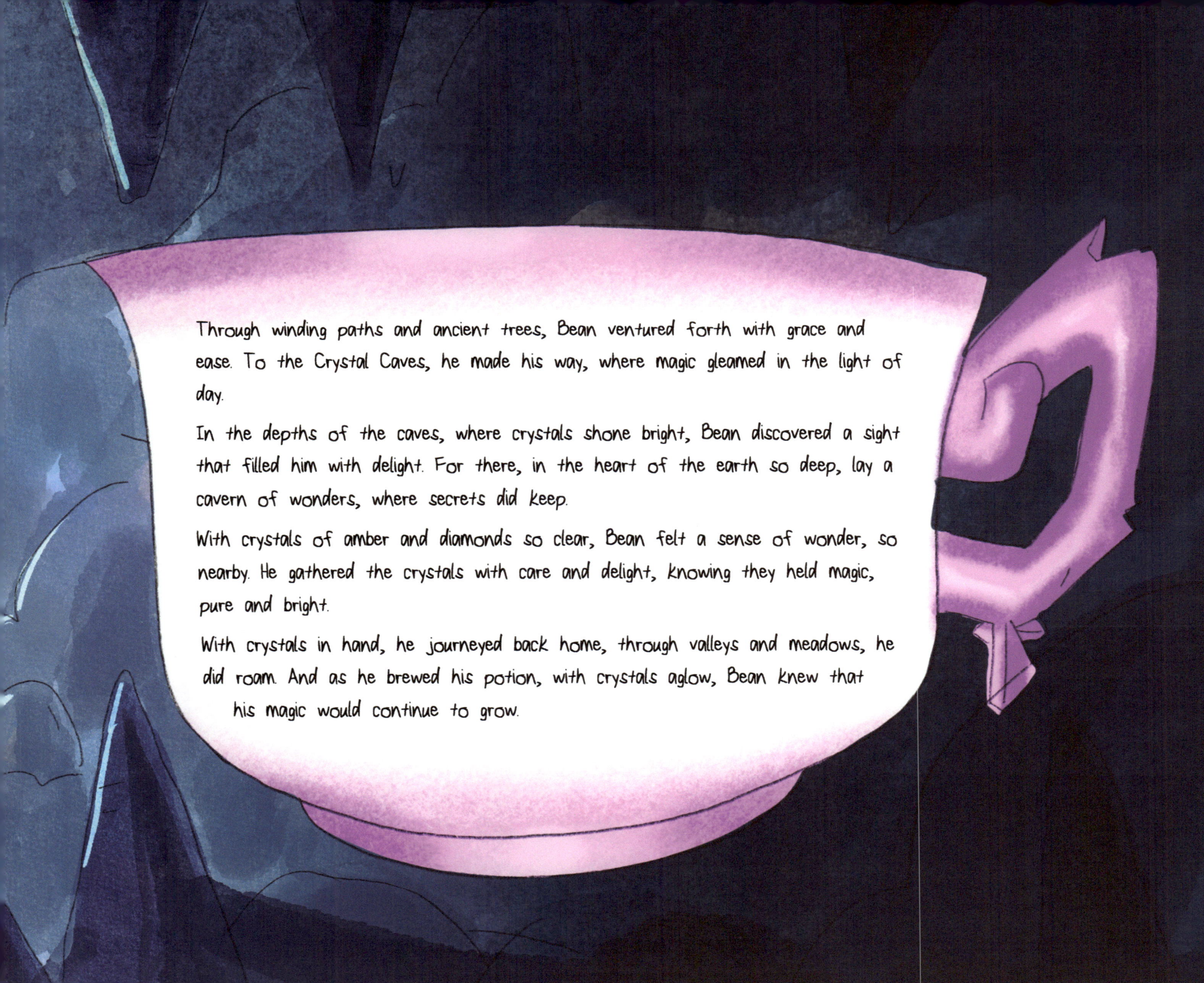

Through winding paths and ancient trees, Bean ventured forth with grace and ease. To the Crystal Caves, he made his way, where magic gleamed in the light of day.

In the depths of the caves, where crystals shone bright, Bean discovered a sight that filled him with delight. For there, in the heart of the earth so deep, lay a cavern of wonders, where secrets did keep.

With crystals of amber and diamonds so clear, Bean felt a sense of wonder, so nearby. He gathered the crystals with care and delight, knowing they held magic, pure and bright.

With crystals in hand, he journeyed back home, through valleys and meadows, he did roam. And as he brewed his potion, with crystals aglow, Bean knew that his magic would continue to grow.

In the heart of the forest, where the fireflies glow, Bean gathered his friends for a joyous show. With laughter and music, they filled the glade, celebrating their bond, so strong and unspayed.

They danced in the moonlight, under the stars, their laughter ringing out, like magical bards. With cups raised high and hearts full of cheer, they toasted to friendship, so precious and dear.

For in each other's company, they found true delight, their spirits lifted, like birds taking flight. With every moment shared, their bond grew strong, and in Bean's enchanted forest, they always belonged.

As the seasons turned and the days grew long, Bean knew it was time to sing his farewell song. For though he loved the forest, with its magic so true, his journey was calling, to adventures anew.

With a heavy heart and a tear in his eye, Bean bid farewell to the trees reaching high. He thanked his friends for their love and their care, and promised to return, whenever they dare.

With a final embrace and a whispered goodbye, Bean spread his wings and took to the sky. As he soared into the sunset, his heart filled with grace, he knew that his adventures would always find their place.

As the sun set on Bean's journey, he looked back with pride, at the lives he had touched, with magic far and wide. With a twinkle in his eye, and a flutter of his wings, Bean knew his story would live on, in the joy that he brings.

For in every cup of coffee, brewed with love and care, lay the promise of a new day, with endless possibilities to share. And though his journey continues, to lands near and far, Bean's magic will always shine, like a morning star.

So, as you sip your coffee, in the morning light, remember Bean the Coffee Fairy, and his magical flight. For though he may be small, his heart is mighty and true, spreading coffee magic, to all who need a brew.

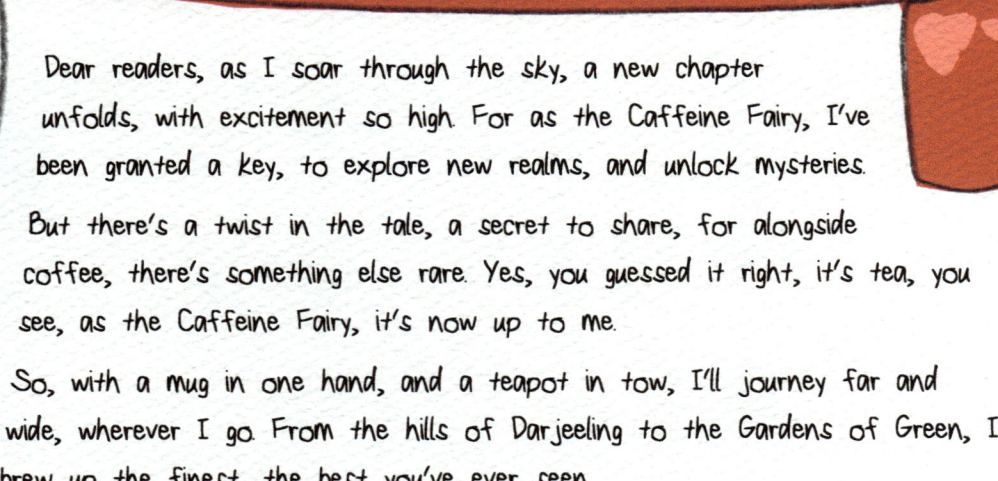

Dear readers, as I soar through the sky, a new chapter unfolds, with excitement so high. For as the Caffeine Fairy, I've been granted a key, to explore new realms, and unlock mysteries.

But there's a twist in the tale, a secret to share, for alongside coffee, there's something else rare. Yes, you guessed it right, it's tea, you see, as the Caffeine Fairy, it's now up to me.

So, with a mug in one hand, and a teapot in tow, I'll journey far and wide, wherever I go. From the hills of Darjeeling to the Gardens of Green, I'll brew up the finest, the best you've ever seen.

But fear not, dear readers, for my love for coffee still burns, in every adventure, in every turn. For whether it's coffee or tea, the magic's the same, to spread joy and warmth, and ignite the flame.

So, here's to new beginnings, to adventures untold, with coffee and tea, my journey unfolds. And though I bid farewell to the forest so dear, I'll carry its magic, wherever I steer.

@BEANTHECOFFEEFAIRY

Welcome to the enchanting world of Bean's Coffee Recipes, where magic meets caffeine in delightful harmony! In this whimsical collection, curated by Bean the Coffee Fairy himself, you'll discover 25 unique and fantastical coffee creations designed especially for adults seeking a taste of adventure with their morning brew.

From frothy concoctions to mystical blends, each recipe is infused with Bean's signature touch of magic, promising to awaken your senses and transport you to a realm of caffeine-fueled wonder. Whether you're a seasoned coffee connoisseur or a curious newcomer to the world of coffee magic, there's something here for everyone to enjoy.

Join Bean on a journey through enchanted forests, mystical caves, and celestial realms as he shares his favorite coffee recipes, each one crafted with love, care, and a sprinkle of fairy dust. So, grab your favorite mug, brew up a cup of Bean's magical elixirs, and prepare to embark on a caffeinated adventure like no other.

Let's brew up some magic together with Bean's Coffee Recipes!

Bean would love to add more recipes to his collection. If you'd like to share your favorite one, click on over to Bean's Instagram page.
Let's see those creative coffees!

Fairy's Frothy Caramel Delight

Ingredients: Espresso, caramel syrup, milk, whipped cream, fairy dust.

Instructions: Brew espresso and stir in caramel syrup. Froth milk and pour over espresso. Top with a generous dollop of whipped cream and sprinkle with fairy dust for an extra touch of magic.

Whimsical White Chocolate Latte

Ingredients: Espresso, steamed milk, white chocolate syrup, whipped cream.

Instructions: Brew espresso and mix with steamed milk and white chocolate syrup. Top with whipped cream.

Enchanted Espresso Martini

Ingredients: Espresso, vodka, coffee liqueur, vanilla syrup.
Instructions: Shake espresso, vodka, coffee liqueur, and vanilla syrup with ice. Strain into a martini glass and garnish with coffee beans.

Mystic Mocha Frappe

Ingredients: Espresso, chocolate syrup, milk, ice, whipped cream, chocolate shavings.
Instructions: Blend espresso, chocolate syrup, milk, and ice until smooth. Pour into a glass, top with whipped cream, and sprinkle with chocolate shavings.

Sparkling Coffee Spritzer

Ingredients: Cold brew coffee, sparkling water, citrus syrup, tonic water.

Instructions: Mix cold brew coffee with sparkling water and citrus syrup. Pour over ice and top with a

splash of tonic water for fizz.

Fairy's Forest Affogato

Ingredients: Vanilla gelato, hot espresso, cocoa powder.

Instructions: Scoop vanilla gelato into a bowl. Pour hot espresso over the gelato and sprinkle with cocoa powder.

Celestial Coconut Cold Brew

Ingredients: Cold brew coffee, coconut milk, coconut syrup, coconut water, ice.

Instructions: Combine cold brew coffee, coconut milk, coconut syrup, and a splash of coconut water. Serve over ice.

Midnight Mocha Milkshake

Ingredients: Espresso, chocolate ice cream, milk, dark chocolate syrup.

Instructions: Blend espresso, chocolate ice cream, milk, and dark chocolate syrup until smooth. Serve in a milkshake glass.

Fairy's Fiery Cinnamon Latte:

Ingredients: Espresso, steamed milk, cinnamon syrup, whipped cream.

Instructions: Brew espresso and mix with steamed milk and cinnamon syrup. Top with whipped cream and a sprinkle of cinnamon.

Dreamy Dalgona Delight

Ingredients: Instant coffee, sugar, hot water, milk, ice.
Instructions: Whisk instant coffee, sugar, and hot water until frothy. Pour over iced milk and stir well.

Chantilly Spray

Istant Coffe

Supernatural Salted Caramel Cold Brew

Ingredients: Cold brew coffee, salted caramel syrup, sea salt.

Instructions: Mix cold brew coffee with salted caramel syrup. Serve over ice and sprinkle with sea salt for extra flavor.

Enigmatic Espresso

Ingredients: Hazelnut gelato, hot espresso, crushed hazelnuts.

Instructions: Place a scoop of hazelnut gelato in a bowl. Pour hot espresso over the gelato and sprinkle with crushed hazelnuts.

Whirling Whipped Coffee

Ingredients: Instant coffee, sugar, hot water, milk, chocolate syrup.

Instructions: Whip instant coffee, sugar, and hot water until frothy. Pour over iced milk and drizzle with chocolate syrup.

Ethereal Eggnog Espresso

Ingredients: Earl Grey tea, espresso, steamed milk, honey.

Instructions: Steep Earl Grey tea and mix with brewed espresso and steamed milk. Sweeten with honey to taste.

Mystic Maple Pecan Latte

Ingredients: Espresso, steamed milk, maple syrup, toasted pecan syrup, cinnamon.

Instructions: Brew espresso and mix with steamed milk, maple syrup, and toasted pecan syrup. Sprinkle with cinnamon.

Cosmic Cold Brew Float

Ingredients: Cold brew coffee, vanilla bean ice cream, root beer.

Instructions: Scoop vanilla bean ice cream into a glass. Pour cold brew coffee over the ice cream and top with root beer.

Fantasy Fig and Honey Latte

Ingredients: Espresso, steamed milk, fig syrup, honey, cinnamon.

Instructions: Brew espresso and mix with steamed milk, fig syrup, and honey. Sprinkle with cinnamon before serving.

Enchanted Earl Grey Latte

Ingredients: Hazelnut gelato, hot espresso, crushed hazelnuts.

Instructions: Place a scoop of hazelnut gelato in a bowl. Pour hot espresso over the gelato and sprinkle with crushed hazelnuts.

Sparkling Strawberry Espresso Tonic

Ingredients: Espresso, tonic water, strawberry syrup, lemon juice, ice.

Instructions: Mix espresso with tonic water, strawberry syrup, and a splash of lemon juice. Serve over ice.

Fairy's Frozen Caramel Macchiato

Ingredients: Espresso, caramel syrup, milk, whipped cream, caramel drizzle.

Instructions: Brew espresso and mix with caramel syrup and milk. Blend with ice until smooth. Top with whipped cream and caramel drizzle.

About the Author

Alex H. Singh is a writer and coffee enthusiast who believes in the power of storytelling to inspire, uplift, and connect us all. When not lost in the world of words, they can be found sipping coffee, exploring new places, or dreaming up the next magical adventure.

About the Illustrator

Fabio Oliveira is an artist with a passion for bringing characters and stories
life through their whimsical illustrations. With a love for detail and a touch of
imagination, they create worlds where anything is possible, from fairy-filled forests to
bustling coffee shops.

And with that, dear reader, we bid you farewell. May your days be filled with laughter,
your nights with dreams, and your cups with the warm embrace of friendship and
coffee.

www.ingramcontent.com/pod-product-compliance
Lightning Source LLC
Chambersburg PA
CBHW040813120626

46547CB00004B/536